Seasons of Goodbye

Seasons of Goodbye

Working Your Way Through Loss

Chris Ann Waters

SORIN BOOKS   Notre Dame, IN

International Standard Book Number: 1-893732-20-7

Library of Congress Catalog Card Number: 00-101263

Cover and text design by Katherine Robinson Coleman

Printed and bound in the United States of America.

To my

grandmother

and

grandfather

who taught me

that through it all,

it is about love.

Contents

ACKNOWLEDGMENTS

Words are tactile. They touch. May these expressions of gratitude reach, respectively,

To God. I could not do anything without your love, strength, and foundation. Thank you for everything. Everything. I love you.

To my agent, Rita Rosenkranz. Your belief in this project was certain from the start and steady to publication. No one else could have guided this book with more diligence, conviction, and care. Deep gratitude to you, Rita.

To those at Sorin Books. *Seasons of Goodbye* has a good home with you from which to travel. Thank you for all guidance and support.

To Candace Abbott for the preparation of this manuscript. As with all you do, the physical skill and spiritual integrity you brought to this work are evident. You are one-of-a-kind, and I am graced to know you.

To those I have met along the way who have encouraged me to share my voice so they could believe in their own. Thank you.

To the patients and families I have had the privilege to meet and serve through Hospice. It is no small irony that when I help others to die well, they help me to live better. Divine reciprocity. May all be served richly by this book.

To Claire Meyer for encouragement and the power of impression.

To my mother, Joan Waters. Strength, dignity, true beauty, and wisdom are gifts you have shared generously with me and each of your children. Thank you for supporting this endeavor, and all I do. My love.

To my father, Michael Waters. Thank you, Dad, for your prayers and faith. Your gift for honest expression aided this work. Your love and encouragement are written throughout. Your love for me is etched on my heart as mine is inscribed on yours.

To Michael, Kelly, James, Todd, Maria, Rosanna, and Ray for being there.

To Matthew for humility and sound judgment.

To Gabriel for determination and skill.

To Victoria for insight and confidence.

To Vincent for inspiration and hope.

To Kirsten for legacy.

To Raymond, Jr., for faith.

To Gabriella for heritage.

To ambassadors of grace: family members and friends. May each of you know the role you have played in helping this book come to fruition. We know where we stand on the journey—together.

Finally, a tender thank you to certain quiet heroes who conduct their lives with such gentle order and integrity that by them dawn is made worthwhile for many. Their train of thought and train of character help keep others moving forward. Their spirit strengthens mine. My cup runneth over.

Chris Ann Waters

Our lives are a series of hellos and goodbyes. The uncertainty in them lies in the length of time between each. However brief or long the span of time between hellos and goodbyes, an end to whatever has begun is natural. It is the order of living things that they begin, have their life, and end.

Seasons of the year teach this as they begin, move with steadiness and patience, and then conclude. Unique features and purposes define each season and bring their exclusive offerings into being. While the seasons bestow a rich plumage of colors, imagery, textures, lessons, and insights, they also bring a clear message with every thaw or harvest: A time shall come when each must change; each must end.

Endings are as much a part of life as beginnings, but the endings are often harder. They place us in unfamiliar territory emotionally, psychologically, and/or physically. We find ourselves in the unknown as a result of the departure of someone or something known, sometimes deeply known. Paradoxically, that which made us feel joyful and secure can also make us feel sorrowful and insecure when gone. Such insecurity and unfamiliarity because of loss brings pain which can be healed only in its own time by the one who bears it, a pain borne by each person in a different way.

Losses take many forms. In addition to physical death, the loss of a friendship, a home, a breast, a job, a pet, or good health are all reasons to grieve. Endings of all types of relationships with people, places, and things challenge us. Finding strength and restoration is the hope and goal for those who grieve. This book was written to help others help themselves reach that goal.

This book came into being as a result of volunteer work I began to do. With a hope others might find what I discovered as a journal writer for many years, I began to work as a volunteer hospice counselor with the intention of helping people write about their feelings regarding life and death, and use writing as a means of closure to serve as a life acknowledgement for themselves and their families; also, to give people a sense of dignity and worth at what is probably the most vulnerable time in life.

Although it was helpful for some patients to write, I found strong receptivity to writing among the bereaved in their efforts to cope with loss. But it didn't end there. After teaching various journal writing classes to all types of groups, I realized that people who weren't even impacted by death in any form (yet or at this point in their lives) still viewed writing with openness because of a need to look inside themselves. I have seen loss present itself in many forms in students' lives. Even though the losses differed, the common denominator among them was to find ways to cope with the loss's offerings. Writing was not "the" answer, but it was "an" answer. This book came as a response to assist them.

While I am not a therapist, social worker, or psychologist, I am a writer. Specifically, I am an individual who has used journal writing to assist me through loss and change. Beginning as a journal writer at the age of twelve when my parents placed a diary in my Easter basket, I learned early on that having a place to write what I was feeling made me feel better. Circumstances didn't change—questions or confusions or delights were still there—but somehow the written record of what I felt validated my feelings and me. I didn't have to go anywhere else, to anyone else, to affirm my experience was real. The journal provided much of what I needed, and it always accepted me—unconditionally—regardless of the tales I came to tell.

Through the journal writing process I have come to glean insights, confidence, and affirmation in a way I do not believe I would have known without written expression. I have written my way through times of sadness, triumphs, and uncertainty.

I know that writing has served to encourage me, define me. I hope this book helps you to receive the same, which is to let writing lead you to discover these offerings for yourself.

Seasons of Goodbye is a companion to support anyone going through a change which involves goodbye. German psychoanalyst Fritz Perls once said, "The only way out is through." This book seeks to help you through. Writing is a coping mechanism, one with therapeutic properties. It is a place to safely, privately, and honestly explore feelings and thoughts. Whether you have written before or have not doesn't matter. You need not be a writer to be helped by this book. Its aim is to acquaint you with skills, tools, ideas, and insights to help yourself. You are met where you are, and it is you who takes yourself where you want to go. The prerequisite for using this book is to have had someone or something removed from your life (or from the life of someone you know) and to seek support and comfort to assist you with this change.

Whatever brought you to this book, although it may feel like an ending, it is a beginning. This is a new place, a new season in your life, one arrived at predictably or unknowingly, but nonetheless unfamiliar. As you stand at this threshold, I hope this book serves as a measure of strength and support as you adjust to the loss and the changes which have ensued. May you find in these pages words and insights that move you to write your own words of truth, healing, and hope to fortify and renew.

It may be hard to believe in tomorrow now that yesterday is gone. But you are trying to believe— you are reading this book. Continue to seek belief in tomorrow. Use all your resources, whatever they may be—spiritual, emotional, physical, therapeutic, other books, family members, friends—to go on so you can go through. Losses in life, however painful and clouded, can bring us to new beginnings and new purposes. At all endings beginnings await. May you discover what those are.

CHAPTER 1

From Hellos to Goodbyes

This is a universe where everything has a price, and we cannot expect to purchase the fragile beauty of love and consciousness without the suffering of transiency and decay.

JOSHUA LOTH LIEBMAN

In its brevity, the word "goodbye" holds a spectrum of emotions as varied as the reasons it is spoken. Our goodbyes are whispered or shouted because of numerous causes. However reasons for goodbye differ from each other, expressions of farewell have one thing in common: change. Goodbye means life is changing and changes include a loss of some kind.

Severed connections, anticipated or unexpected, affect people of every age throughout every stage of life. Whatever form losses take, whether they be people, places, or situations, they are experiences we feel because of an attachment to someone or something.

Losses come in many forms because relationships do. Loss of a spouse, a child, a friend due to death; loss of a healthy body; a home deeply loved that has been sold or destroyed in a fire; the end of a special friendship or intimate relationship; or a career ended to retirement were all living relationships.

Similarly, a camper, a sailboat enjoyed for years through unforgettable sunsets and storms, a room with a favored object such as a carpenter's workbench or a sewing machine, a sport, a craft, a book, a garden, a crib, a piece of jewelry, a dress, or a uniform are things we can have a relationship with and mourn when circumstances alter our association and bring them to a conclusion. Our interactions with humans are not the only "living" relationships we develop.

We become related to people and things by what we exchange with them. By giving of ourselves to someone or something and receiving in return, a relationship is born. Objects come to breathe because we breathe life into them. This breath comes from the heart, and it is the heart that is at the center of all living relationships.

Hearts are affected deeply by loss because it arrives with more frequency these days. Although goodbyes have always been and shall continue to be a prevailing thread in life's fabric, goodbyes are more prevalent today. Relationships with people and things are shortened, making the experience of goodbye closer to one another.

We meet goodbyes more often for many reasons: diseases, i.e., cancer, AIDS, heart disease, Alzheimer's; divorce; drugs; natural disasters; terrorism; abortion; widespread teenage pregnancy, accompanied by loss of youth; violence, terminating life prematurely; and socioeconomic circumstances that result in emotional, psychological, or physical challenges or fatalities. All of these are in addition to natural endings.

Furthermore, our goodbyes are experienced as a result of the transient nature of life in contemporary society. Plentiful choices regarding

What, after all, is more personal than suffering?

THOMAS MERTON

lifestyles, professions, and locations contribute to abbreviated relationships. New jobs in other states and countries disengage many relationships; competition for goals, professional and personal, often requires a focus on primary intentions which detracts from other concentrations. The vast options available to creative living offer a magnitude of choices that are made while goodbyes are being spoken. Life moves quickly today and, as a result, many relationships are short-lived.

But, however short or long a relationship is, its length by no means determines its value. A brief relationship, as well as one enduring over many years, has the power to make us grieve. It is all a question of how much of an impact a relationship has on us, how meaningful its message.

Depending upon the degree of attachment to the loss, some changes can be exceedingly difficult. When someone or something of deep significance departs, life becomes a reality we may not recognize or do not want to accept. This reality can be profoundly trying, particularly when reasons for goodbyes are tragic, painful, and seemingly premature. The void left because of some goodbyes can seem impossible to fill. Losses can be wrenching, heartbreaking, and confusing, and coping through them among the greatest feats we face as human beings. Such goodbyes try our

I will turn their mourning into joy, and will comfort them, and make them rejoice from their sorrow.

JEREMIAH 31:13 (KJV)

every cell, making it immensely difficult to combat reality's force.

If goodbyes are so difficult, why give attention to them by trying to write through them? The answer is simple: so we can say hello.

Hello is a worthwhile destination even though some trips there are arduous. Hello is a place to discover, a place where new truths are learned, new visions are seen, where hope abounds. It is the place where we first entered that brought us to this end we now experience in our loss. And while goodbyes are painful, the wondrous thing about hello is that even though one experience ends, new hellos truly have no end. We can begin again and again for as long as we choose to.

Life is a never-ceasing cycle in which the ebb and flow of beginnings and endings are in motion. Through these starts and finishes life unfolds. Even though goodbye is the underside of hello, it is the steppingstone from which new hellos are reached. Until goodbye is uttered, new beginnings cannot be clearly met.

But, in order to meet hello again, we must go through the changes goodbye brings. The joint arrival of change and goodbye can be penetrating and challenging as attempts are made to let go of something in an effort to receive something else. Before a hello can be considered, it is necessary

There must be something strangely sacred in salt. It is in our tears and in the sea.

KAHLIL GIBRAN

to release from one way of being to move toward a way of becoming.

Release is not always easy, nor is saying goodbye. It is difficult to leave our yesterdays, for we want to take them with us into tomorrow. But there isn't room for yesterday in tomorrow. There is only room for parts of yesterday, which is its essence. This we can take. What we leave behind is the rest, and this must be done in order to make room for new gifts. Life has so much to give. Its gifts are limitless, and it wants to keep giving for as long as we are able to receive. For each to receive there must be room. We must be open. Openness is there when we are able to say goodbye.

As hard as losses and goodbyes are, in our humanness we are amazing. We discover, albeit incrementally, strength within and fresh eyes with which to see our world when we didn't think such a view was possible or even desirable. This day-to-day continuance of all of life, to which we are still connected even though we experienced a loss, makes us part of life's daily unfolding and progression. Without realizing it, in our state of shock, numbness, busyness—whatever our condition due to changeful goodbyes—we are taking part in the evolution of ourselves and our destinies, as well as life as a

And these losses are necessary because we grow by losing and leaving and letting go.

JUDITH VIORST

whole. And within this participation, however weak or unclear, advancement is occurring.

In these subtle forward movements lies our strength and hope. Here, whether by admission or reluctance, will come our gradual yet steady opportunity for acceptance of the present reality of our lives. Here is where we can enter into writing to help us adjust to this new reality.

Enlightenment begins on the other side of despair.

JEAN-PAUL SARTRE

CHAPTER 2

Beginnings

WHEN SHALL I BEGIN?

Shall I begin in Autumn?
    when the color of change is clear
    in crisp air
    in lessening light.
Shall I begin in Winter?
    when beginnings seem few
    in the sun's brief appearance
    in the deepest nights.
Shall I begin in Spring?
    with the daffodils
    in brighter light
    in freer movement.
Shall I begin in Summer?
    in warmth
    in lingering sunshine
    in endless days.
When shall I begin
    to understand, to care
    offering words of truth,
    encouraging my thoughts
    when will I need these most?
When shall I begin?

    Perhaps I shall begin now.

Whether you are a writer or have never written before does not matter. It does not matter. Neither does punctuation, grammar, or spelling. The writing you will be doing is a method to be used for coping through transition. These writings are your private recordings to be evaluated by no one, to be shared with no one, if this is your choice.

What you are doing is creating a confidential, respected, and readily accessible place to go at any time where, quietly and honestly, you can express what you are feeling. It is not a place for judgment or criticism, even from yourself. A journal is a haven and a means of support to help you adjust to the changes taking place in your life. There are no right or wrong answers in journal entries or exercises. The responses will be as individual as your fingerprints, so don't expect to find "right" outcomes. There aren't any. But there is truth. And in this truth shall come release and relief.

About This Book

Ahead are four chapters leading you through the four seasons of the year: autumn, winter, spring, and summer. The natural seasons illustrate the seasons of change as we move through them to goodbye. Below is a brief guide indicating each season's purpose regarding change.

. . . since I think best with a pencil in my hand, I started naturally to write.

ANNE MORROW
LINDBERGH

Autumn	The pivotal point of change.
Winter	Getting still and introspective. Remembering yesterday.
Spring	Regaining hope. Letting go.
Summer	Participating again in life with acceptance, peace and new purpose.

This is what I learned: That everybody is talented, original and has something important to say.

BRENDA UELAND

You can begin reading this book at any time of year, at any point in the change you are going through. You need not read or do the exercises following the natural seasons—the movements of your change and the unfolding of seasons outside your window may not coincide.

If you do not live in a region where the change in seasons is dramatic, use your understanding of the change in seasons to apply the changes in your environment to the changes in your life. While the way each individual moves through the cycle of change differs, the cycle itself is the same and places all of us on the same ground when it is experienced.

Begin reading the book from the beginning and in sequence. At whatever point you are in the cycle of change, you will probably find yourself staying in that chapter longer. Let your feelings guide you as to when you should settle into one place longer or move on.

Another point to consider is that this book can be used after you have gone through a full cycle of change. Even though time has passed and we may think we are beyond the effects of loss and have said goodbye, sometimes we have not. The readings and exercises can be valuable and healing long after you or someone you know has experienced loss, just as they are beneficial when loss is fresh. Furthermore, there may be times in your life when you want to revisit a specific chapter and do the exercises again. Follow your inclination. If you feel led to do a winter exercise even through you are living through a summer heart, do a winter exercise. There must be something in your soul that needs to focus there. Let it.

Keep this in mind throughout the reading of this book: Even though "writing fruits" are picked by tending the garden pages each day, do not feel you must perform. Establishment of any relationship should be of one's own volition; this is certainly true of such an intimate relationship as one with a journal. Therefore, let writing be an experience you come to freely and willingly so it can offer you freedom rather than making you feel harnessed. Brenda Ueland explains in her book *If You Want to Write* that when we are writing we "should not be like Lord Byron on a mountain top, but like a child stringing beads in kindergarten." Let it come out naturally, and it will.

Truth has no special time of its own. Its hour is now— always.

ALBERT SCHWEITZER

. . . if you do not express your own original ideas, if you do not listen to your own being, you will have betrayed yourself.

ROLLO MAY

If you read this entire book and still have not written one word, so be it. One day when you are ready to write, you will. When you are prepared, you will see your first words, first fruits. If you force your hand you'll force your heart, which may not be ready to articulate its feelings yet. Let it come out freely. Just as nothing in nature is forced, truths cannot be forced. They come in their own time, and that timing is always perfect. Your freest writing may come months or years after you have read this book. When you are ready, the page will be waiting; then you will be ready to go there and let yourself go.

Similarly, since you know how you feel and what you are inclined to do, while you are encouraged to write often, only you can know when to begin and when to continue. As you move along in this book, there are exercises at the end of each seasonal chapter. You are invited to do the exercises as you feel ready. Only you know when that is.

For example, you may find you are not prepared to do winter exercises if you are still in an autumn frame of heart. This is valid. Keep reading. When you are ready to go back and do the exercises, you will know. At that time, return to a specific chapter you are prepared to explore, and then begin the exercises.

You may want to read the entire book first and then go back and participate in the exercises. Do so. Linger wherever you feel certain feelings need attention. Don't rush exercises. Indulge the need of your heart to meander in a certain place. Need is accompanied by reason. There is a reason you feel more moved in one season or another. It is telling you where you are. Listen to what your heart is saying and then follow those thoughts with words.

Preparations: Choosing a Journal

When you write in response to the exercises in the book and/or journal entries elicited from your own list of ideas (which is discussed further on), it is best to go to the same place to write. In this way, the physical sight and touch of the same pages creates a bond. Also, it is good to have your writing gathered in the same place. It keeps something in your life organized while you are feeling fragmented.

Choosing a journal is the first step to creating a place to write. A journal is no more than a pad or book of paper. This choice can be as simple as a spiral-bound loose-leaf notebook, or a fabric-covered journal which is sold in stationery or book stores. Also, a sketch pad can serve as a journal. Sketch pads, which are sold in art supply

All writing begins in the sea of experience.

BARRY LANE

or stationery stores, are a preferred type of journal for some people because they don't have any lines and the open pages invite freer expression.

Personal choice is the same for writing implements. Get yourself a simple ballpoint pen or a fine point marker. Whatever works for you. I do not suggest using pencils. With pencils there is an inclination to erase truthful words away. We want to save our truths so they remain indelibly on our hearts and continue to offer guidance and healing.

The choice is yours. Choose whatever types of materials make you feel comfortable. The amount of writing you do will, in all likelihood, require other journals. You can choose the same style as before or something different. Whatever you want to use, use. Just keep writing, and keep your writing in chronological order. In years to come, you may want to look back and see the progress you have made through endings to beginnings.

In various journal courses I have taught, I have had students come to me and tell me they are apprehensive about saving their journals. They worry they will be found. This is a valid concern. If your dwelling place doesn't offer respectful privacy, it is reason to postpone, if not completely

It is only with the heart that one can see rightly; what is essential is invisible to the eye.

ANTOINE DE
SAINT-EXUPÉRY

hinder, written expression. But there are ways around this.

First, try to write somewhere other than at home—a library, a friend's house, your workplace, a park, your car. If you have a trusted relative or friend with whom you can keep your journal, store it there. It is good to preserve your writings for future reference. However, if this is not possible, I advise you to still write journal entries, but rip them up and throw them away after you have written them. While saving pieces is preferable, the opportunity to voice yourself and air what is going on inside of you is just as effective, regardless of whether entries are torn or saved. Just write. However and wherever you can do it, do it.

A word about computers. Given today's highly sophisticated technology, computers may be preferred "writing instruments." If this is your choice, fine. However, it is highly recommended that you use paper and pen. There is something far more personal and textural about the paper and pen in hand which assists expression. A pen in hand gliding along the paper connects you physically with the output, the tangible result. You are touching what you write the moment you express it in your journal.

Natalie Goldberg, writer and teacher, offers in her book *Wild Mind*, "I do all my original writing by

. . . listen to what your inner world is saying.

JOYCE RUPP

hand. I have greater mobility. . . . Plus it feels more connected with my body; my hand moves with my arm and shoulder, which is connected to my chest and heart. All good writing comes from the body and is a physical experience."

Furthermore, paper and pen are portable and travel easily. Even if you have a portable laptop computer you like to use or must use at times, once you become comfortable writing and need this place, the easy accessibility and portability of a journal (necessary for some exercises) will support your writing better.

With the tools you have chosen, the practice of writing has the potential to become sharper and telling. When practiced, it comes to be trusted. The effectiveness to be discovered in writing is found when we participate in the process. Writing reveals its benefits when we are involved. This involvement comes from an investment of time and self. When you are ready to write, writing will be ready to meet you where you are.

Using Your Journal: Coming to the Page

Before we talk about what to write, there are a few guidelines to keep in mind about how to write. When starting out, it is good to select a set time and place. Choose a time and place which is relatively free from interruptions. This

. . . the self who emerges on paper is a far stiffer person than the one who sat down.

WILLIAM ZINSSER

establishes two things: a writing habit begins, and a physical place for expression is designated in your day. This is time you give to you. You go to the journal, but you are really going to yourself.

When you go to your journal to write, a good way to start writing is by using a common writing practice known as freewriting. Freewriting is simply being free to write down whatever you want without any concern for the outcome. Suspend all logical forms of sentence structure, tone, style, or result. Concerns about grammar, punctuation, and spelling are abandoned. This releases you from considering the do's and don'ts of writing, freeing you to get down to what is important—whatever is on your heart and mind at the time.

As you let your mind follow the pen, which is always moving forward, don't look back. Stay with the flow of what you are writing. When it gets powerful you may sometimes get scared and stop. This may happen from time to time. It is the energy and emotion coming out. At first it can be unwanted, but gradually you will come to feel it and go with it, and even welcome it.

There are different ways to get started when it is time to write in your journal, in addition to the exercises and prompts in this book. You may have a fierce emotion clawing at you, or there may have been a particular event that day, fresh

The writer is more concerned to know than to judge.

W. Somerset Maugham

What is real, and does it hurt?

THE VELVETEEN RABBIT

on your heart, you want to express. Either of these will lead you to begin writing. During times of change we are more vulnerable and, therefore, more sensitive. It is likely that, during the course of the day and night, ordinary events will take on different meaning. Whatever becomes a focal point in your day, let it be the point from which you start to write. This event serves as your writing beginning for that day.

Writing Is Emotional

Journal writing comes from the heart, not the mind. When writing is truthful, expect all sorts of emotions to emerge. Just as they stir within you, they will present themselves on the page. Expect tears, laughter, confusion, anger. All of these are common reactions, and they are necessary to experience in order to heal, to understand. Loss and change put us on an emotional roller coaster and these emotions will vary from hour to hour, day to day. Yet, no matter how you feel, you are encouraged to come to the page.

Come to the page when you feel low, when you feel empty, when energy is limp and you think you have little to say. Still come. Come when you are crying because of something you remembered, something you thought you had forgotten. Come to the page when you are angry and you want to yell, or when you are happy and you want to savor the feeling. Coming to your journal means entering a place to write whatever you are feeling. You mustn't think you should be of a certain frame of mind to write. Change is not about a certain frame of mind; it is about many minds. Within change, moods alter depending upon primary emotions dwelling in the heart. What you are doing when you come to your journal is channeling your feelings to a place where they are expressed and removed from you. Kimberly Snow, in *Writing Yourself Home*, writes, "Don't feel bad about what you have written . . . by writing it all, you're revealing emotions and thoughts that can help you figure out the big picture of your life."

When you write your feelings out, you seek to understand them. But, even if you don't understand them and they seem muddled, when you write you show you care enough about yourself to try to understand and cleanse yourself of confusion. This is a significant move forward to saying goodbye. Taking emotion from within, that has the power to bridle advancement, is a big step ahead. In this act, you seek to place emotions elsewhere, in a safe place. This place is one you can come to trust to be there for as long as you need and want to go there. How long will this be? That is hard to answer. Everyone finds their release from issues of loss in their own way and in their own time. Healing is the objective. But bear in mind that the extent to which you try to

A journey of a thousand miles must begin with a single step.

LAO-TZU

> *It is not possible for anyone to embrace truth except in proportion to his readiness for it.*
>
> JOEL GOLDSMITH

> *You must do the thing you think you cannot do.*
>
> ELEANOR ROOSEVELT

heal yourself is the extent to which healing shall reach you.

Healing is as penetrating as we are open and honest. Being truthful about feelings—all feelings, even the best ones—is scary. And when these are put in writing there is something so obvious, clear, even glaring at times, about them which mirrors who we are that can be uncomfortable, for both beginning and seasoned writers. Yet writing is a place of acceptance, and when you continually go there to express yourself, you build trust. You come to find that you can go to the page more openly because of its openness to you.

Acceptance you receive in the journal as you write is most important. Here you will find acceptance of yourself, flaws and all, which is fine because everyone is flawed—*everyone*—no matter how perfectly some people seem to glide through life. Humanity and imperfection go hand in hand. It will never be any other way. Still, it takes courage to admit our weaknesses to ourselves. When we write our truths they are a reflection of who we are. Even though we may not always like who we are, when we trust the page and write out what we think and feel, we find freedom. We become liberated from expectations and masks either we ourselves or others impose. We learn by expressing who we are, we become free to be who we are.

Reaching this place, we learn that through all our beginnings, endings, and in-betweens, this freedom enables us to spend life doing more genuine living rather than expending energy denying or disguising weaknesses. It is okay to be angry or to cry as much as it is to laugh. Expressing and accepting emotions as changes from loss warrants allows us to be what we are in the face of change—nothing more than human. The page knows this and accepts us. It is we who must accept ourselves. And to accept ourselves—all we've done, all we haven't done, all we've said, all we've left unspoken—is to say, "I am human." We all are.

So relax. As you begin to read through the seasons and participate in exercises, or just go to your journal with your own thoughts, don't be intimidated by a blank piece of paper. You'll fill it up, and many more once you get comfortable with the process and realize writing is a friend. Be your true self. Be honest. And remember that here, no matter what you are feeling, writing will never betray you; it will always accept you.

Keeping a journal while you are going through the tunnel of change is to have a beam guiding your way to the greater light. Tunnels have a beginning and an ending. It is important to

Only that day dawns to which we are awake.

HENRY DAVID THOREAU

remember we enter them from light and exit them to light. While we are going through, we must keep going no matter how dim our view, because the end is where the light is, just as it was in the beginning.

CHAPTER 3

Autumn

The Colors of Change

Leaves of change

    fall to the earth

    returning to where roots begin.

Natural wonders transform every second

    Humanity cries

    expecting something different.

Time moves forward

    Are past hours redeemed?

Colors of life swirl

    as hearts rustle

Change does not take

    Yesterday it leaves.

Vibrance, activity, and, most vividly, "change" depict the season of autumn. Leaves transform from shades of green to a kaleidoscope of color. Daylight lessens. Air becomes crisper. The gentleness of summer recedes. It is a time of movement, dramatic in contrast to the long, warm, settled days of summer. Maturity crests, fullness begins to fade, and it is time to pick fruits, ripened or damaged, to begin growth for a future harvest.

Leaves float in abandon, drifting downward from emptying branches, branches where leaves came to be. Limbs, once radiant with color, become bare as growth descends. Autumn reveals visual magnificence while offering this candid truth: Everything as we know it now will not remain as it is.

Change. As unwanted, uncomfortable, and unfamiliar as it can be, it is as much a part of life as the sun, rain, and air we breathe. It is a certainty in life, a truth never to alter. All living things are constantly in motion since change is in operation every moment. As natural creatures, humans continuously move, never staying in the same place. It is impossible to remain stationary since we are alive and, therefore, part of the ongoing cycle of nature which is never at a standstill.

Yet nature's productions, and particularly removal of results, evokes sadness and can even

And the heaven gave rain, and the earth brought forth her fruit.

James 5:18 (KJV)

All changes, even the most longed for, have their melancholy; for what we leave behind us is a part of ourselves; we must die to one life before we can enter into another.

ANATOLE FRANCE

seem destructive rather than progressive. But change is progressive, and nowhere is this more evident than in nature where change, subtle or bold but ever extraordinary, invites beginnings. Progress requires movement. Though movement appears as an ending at times, in actual fact, endings are the necessary agents for forward movement.

Much change goes on discreetly. However, it is the pivotal moments in which change manifests when its effects are clearly seen and fully experienced. While every second leads to pivotal moments (and each subsequent moment supports the adjustment to a specific change while simultaneously preparing us for the next one to come), it is in these actual moments when reality as we have known it shifts, that we realize we must shift, too, even though we may not wish to.

All types of changes are disturbing on one level or another, even welcome changes. These impose a variety of heightened emotions we are never quite prepared for. Not knowing where change will lead us physically, emotionally, mentally, or spiritually, change always invites us into the unknown which can be frightening. To be on the brink of welcome change is scary. Arriving at this precipice, although reached willingly, can still engender unsettled feelings. How could it not—this is a new place being experienced for the first time.

But it is only when we venture into the unknown—the first times—that we have the opportunity to make discoveries and to grow. Change holds seeds in its hands. When or if these seeds will flourish remains a choice each individual makes. We are the gardeners of our lives, and it is up to each of us to choose to plant the seeds change gives to us.

Two Types of Change

Change arrives in one of two ways: expectedly and unexpectedly. Either arrival brings with it an assortment of differences to be coped with and adjusted to. Whatever way change meets us, it is always accompanied by a goodbye of some kind.

When change comes expectedly as a result of a choice that includes something new and hopeful such as a home, a marriage, a child, or career change, we welcome newness in our lives. But even when change is our choice, there is an odd sadness in welcome hellos. This sadness is the echo of yesterday which must be left behind. It is the shedding of leaves to prepare for new growth. Leaving yesterday accommodates today, so we must say goodbye to what has been to allow for what is to be.

Yesterdays hold within them tremendous attachment. They are the familiar and we gravitate toward that which we know, sometimes regardless

Birth and death are the two noblest expressions of bravery.

KAHLIL GIBRAN

Let mourning stop when one's grief is fully expressed.

CONFUCIUS

of our like or dislike of this known place. Still, newness is compelling, and, when we choose to make transitions going from the known to the unknown, we are choosing change in spite of discomforting feelings. In essence, we are choosing growth.

While seeds of growth are available in all change, the ability to see these seeds may be shrouded when change is of the other type, unexpected. Abrupt and deeply trying change keeps seedlings concealed, sometimes for a very long time. A family watching a loved one debilitate slowly from illness, those who lose a loved one in a sudden accident, or a family shattered by divorce grope with heartache inherent in such difficult losses. As persons cope with the anguish such experiences bring, the ability to see beginnings is naturally blinded by grief.

Meeting change due to tragedy, difficulty, and circumstances beyond our control is a tremendous challenge which might literally throw us into a whirlwind of emotion. Such crises bring stark and burdensome truths to hearts and minds that are barely understood, let alone accepted for a long time to come.

Still, whatever we face in life, acceptance is the goal. Accepting where we are, where we have been, to arrive at where we stand, is the task before us. As living members of nature, we are meant to continue, no matter what has changed in our individual lives to bring us to our present place. This is the place we must come to recognize, understand, and accept. This may be difficult. Accepting where we are is aided by accepting how we feel as a result of loss and change. Feelings are valid—all feelings—whatever colors they reveal. Recognizing and respecting varying feelings offers meaningful insight to the reality of loss as well as a way by which we are moved toward saying goodbye.

Emotional Foliage

The colors of loss include a broad range of hues that filter into the days and nights of transition. Never knowing which colors will appear, it is uncertain which colors will pervade our consciousness at any given time. The arrival of various emotions and how long we will experience them are unpredictable. When we are going through adjustments, we can rest, knowing we cannot be sure of what color our hearts will reflect from one day or one hour to the next.

Loss is a rainbow of colors that fall about the heart, cluttering it with emotions. It can be: black and unwanted, gray and confusing, red and angry, blue and detached, green and remorseful. It comes in subtle pastels, ever so gentle differences in daily routines and patterns that make us remember what we may prefer to forget. Or, it

Just as acceptance has its rewards, nonacceptance has its penalties.

ARTHUR GORDON

The human heart has hidden treasures, in secret kept, in silence sealed.

CHARLOTTE BRONTË

arrives in dramatic strokes of forgiveness or regret, reminding us of our humanness, our fragility, our need to rely on a strength beyond our own.

There is not one specific color to describe loss, not one singular emotion. Since losses are such emotionally charged experiences, moods shift often. While these altered states are confusing, they are to be expected when going through transition. This vibrant reality is one that colors our individual worlds with a message: When change comes, we are asked to color the experience with understanding, and we are asked to prepare for something new.

Shedding Understanding

While autumn leaves cascade to the ground, moving from branches that once held them securely, their descent to the earth's surface makes them part of it again. Leaves, matured by the strength of each season, become dry and crumpled, only to sprinkle their crisp remnants over soil in preparation for new growth. Looking unnecessary in their decayed state, it would appear they have been brought to an end. But appearances are deceptive. Although withered leaves depict endings, in the course of nature there is purpose in all. It is from here a new beginning stems.

Nature is always preparing. When leaves fall, nature uses fragmented foliage of the past to till the soil that will grow life anew in due season. Human eyes see departure, nature's only progress. Endings support beginnings. And while nature uses its resources to repeat the cycle over and over again, likewise, endings that occur in our lives can be used to support something new.

On a cold Sunday morning in late autumn, I looked out my living room window and saw that the lake in front of my home had thawed overnight. The only exception was a large ice formation to the east. Seagulls visited from the ocean nearby and landed on this ice island. They rested there while they watched the lake's movement from the frozen perch.

This silver piece of ice in the lake added dimension to the usual, complacent flow of water. My eyes were drawn to this conspicuous barrier which, in its stoic stance, offered a provocative view of the lake. I didn't want it to melt. I didn't want it to change. But it would change, for nothing stays the same.

Changes in life, whether the result of endings prolonged, expected, cold, relieving, cruel, tragic, or welcome, remove something from our lives to clear a place for something new. As trees in autumn shed their limbs of all their foliage, which includes the most beautiful along with the

Our life is an apprenticeship to the truth that around every circle another can be drawn; that there is no end in nature, but every end is a beginning; that there is always another dawn risen on mid-noon, and under every deep a lower deep opens.

RALPH WALDO EMERSON

All that we do is done with an eye to something else.

ARISTOTLE

immature, it must let everything go to prepare itself for new growth. It cannot hold on to its fruit, for if it does there would be no progress, no chance to move beyond now and let tomorrow come to bear new fruit, a tomorrow whose fruits shall take another cycle for nature to create.

While it is sad to witness leaves fall, knowing a season has come to an end, nature, like life, always has something special ahead. As autumn departs, winter prepares to offer its hidden crystal treasures.

WRITING ABOUT YOUR LOSS

Go to your journal and write about the loss in your life. What has changed? How? Has someone died? Has a relationship reached an end? Have you or has someone in your life become ill? Retirement? A relocation?

Whatever it is in your life that has changed, describe this experience. Write about the details that led to it if it was an anticipated event. Write the details as you remember them when your world turned upside down due to an unexpected change. Be as specific as possible. Write for as long as it takes. Write for twenty minutes or an hour. However long you need, take the time.

AUTUMN IMAGE TRIGGERS

In Barry Lane's book *Writing as a Road to Self-Discovery*, he talks about triggers—things that spur thoughts and help us begin to write. I am getting you started to write by providing what I call "image triggers." For every seasonal chapter in this book there is a list of image triggers. These are words for you to read and then write whatever they bring to mind. These are brief lists. Every season will have specific images to be recalled, i.e., names of people, places, or objects that hold special meaning for you. Add them to each season list as you think of them.

As you read the list and one image triggers various memories, go to your journal and explore where this one image takes you. Follow it through to the details and feelings it brings to heart and mind. Take as much time and as many pages as you need in your journal to follow the image. You may find that one word evokes such special meaning that you may choose to do just this one exercise for the day and explore another tomorrow. The decision is yours. Write as you are led.

Remember: Every single occurrence in your life, however common, is an experience you, only you, can describe. Whatever images come to mind are reflections of the experience the way you perceived it. However you want to express that experience in words, you have the right and privilege to do so. So do it.

AUTUMN IMAGE TRIGGERS   *Add Your List Here*

pumpkin farms

burning leaves   _____

chrysanthemums   _____

hot cider and donuts   _____

Halloween   _____

apple strudel   _____

mothballs   _____

first day of school   _____

football   _____

hayrides   _____

blackboards   _____

wheelbarrows   _____

raking leaves   _____

Thanksgiving _____

squash _____

flannel shirts _____

stadium blankets _____

_____

DIALOGUE WITH CLOTHING

Think of an article of clothing that was part of the loss you experienced. Was it something you wore? Perhaps it was a dress, a suit, a hat, or scarf. Was it something someone wore who was involved in your loss? Is it just a favorite article of clothing that has been with you for years? I have a navy blue sweatshirt that I love. It has been with me for many years, has lived through lots of beach days, has traveled many places. It has lots of stories to tell.

Step out of your own mind and into the mind of your special article of clothing. Dialogue with it and let it remember significant details of change or events it has known. Let the clothing monopolize the conversation. Listen to what it tells you. Yes, you can ask it questions and offer comments. But don't interfere with its voice. Let it speak. Let yourself learn by listening to another version of yesterday's account. Take as much time as the article of clothing wants to take. Dialogues will be for as long as the clothing has something to say. Stay with it.

COLORING EMOTIONS

PART I

Take a box of crayons or colored pencils. You don't need too many. A few will do. Either go to your journal and draw the diagram below or take a sheet of blank paper and draw it. Write one word in the center circle that describes your loss. Look at the colors you have to color with as if they were your emotions. Don't generalize colors. Yellow may be happy for you, or it may not. Now, take your crayons and color in the pie shapes according to how you feel about the loss and change in your life. You may find you use one color to fill in the entire pie. Or, you may use just two colors, or a dozen. Also, you may leave parts of the pie blank because you don't know how you feel. Color it in according to what you feel is a reflection of your emotions at this time.

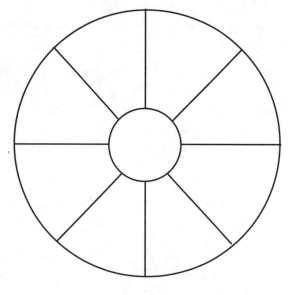

Go to your journal and give your colors words. Interpret what the colors mean to you and why you think you chose them. Did you use several colors but more of one? Explain why.

PART III

At the end of each seasonal chapter, do this exercise. Compare the colors you use from drawing to drawing to see if you choose different colors or if you use more or less of one color. Go to your journal and write about what these colors say to you now.

DESCRIBING YOURSELF IN COLORS

PART I

Below is a list of colors. As you read the colors, think of the emotions you associate with them. While some colors typically liken themselves to a particular emotion (i.e., yellow often implies happiness), for each person each color really holds a different meaning. Blue and gray are two of my most favorite colors, making me feel comfort, warmth, and peace. But some people would associate blue and gray with sadness. To each his own.

This is a partial list. There are many colors to describe feelings. Some colors are soft, some are strong, just like feelings. As you think of other colors you want to add, extend the list. In addition to the exercise below, think of using colors when you begin a journal entry for the day. Sometimes thinking about how you feel enables you to explore why you feel this way.

Red	Silver	Pink
Amber	Turquoise	Sienna
Green	Orange	Apricot
Yellow	Black	Fuchsia
Purple	Taupe	Gray
White	Blue	Gold
Copper	Magenta	Brown

PART II

Go back to the first exercise, "Writing About Your Loss."
Think about the events and use colors to describe how you felt
during the loss and how you feel now. Begin to write about the
event again, using colors to describe your feelings. Be as clear in
your description of your feelings (moods) as you can be. Don't
be afraid to write that you feel black if you do. Black can be a
dark, unwanted emotion, but it is as valid and acceptable as
pink. Let yourself express whatever it is that your personal loss
caused you to feel. Be true to your colors; they reflect the reality of the loss as you experienced it. There are no wrong colors,
no wrong answers; be honest. Take as much time as you need.

CHAPTER 4

Winter

Darkness Casts Its Own Light

Blankets of safety
are folded about
yesterday's gifts.
A winter heart protects
its treasures.
No cold penetrates
the past.
Within a winter heart
memories breathe
still.

Long dark nights blending with brief sunlit days, strong winds, and icy layers covering settled soil mark winter. Frigid temperatures prevail as the earth's landscape is traced with silver and white highlights. Winter arrives. It draws a striking contrast against vibrant autumn fruitage now gone to vacate the land for winter's stay.

During this quiet period of winter's visitation, lonesome are the days and nights through this season of change. When goodbyes bring sadness there is no sense of moving forward. Weight of departure presses against the future, unyielding. Suns and moons spill over each other and time takes on a strange new meaning. Time is not. Its familiar concept used to structure activities loses its framework. Time seems frozen like the winter land itself.

In the somber months of winter slumber, blooms of spring rest and wait their turn as nature trusts its own timing. Nature is patient. All comes into being for a reason, and development is supported by every step, however small, weak, or quiet. Far too resourceful and purposeful, nature makes use of all it produces. Numb land is the foundation on which spring blossoms will ascend in due time. Winter is the surface beneath which that ascent begins.

With eyes and ears distracted by cold and ice, we cannot see what is taking place under the ground.

My sun sets to rise again.

ROBERT BROWNING

> *Saturn was sometimes called sol niger, the black sun. In his darkness there is to be found a precious brilliance, our essential nature, distilled by depression as perhaps the greatest gift of melancholy.*
>
> THOMAS MOORE

It would appear that in its solid state t here is no progress in the making. In periods of transition that are sullen it seems we, too, are not advancing. But, while the pace of nature slows in winter, it does not cease. Future growth is being supported in this season of preparation where a silent turn in the cycle, an essential turn, is at the fore.

My mother has always been sensitive to nature's changes. When my sister, brothers, and I were growing up, I remember my mother stopping our activities to tell us to come to the window to watch the sun set, to see the fog roll in or out, or to watch the snow fall. When it was wintertime, we were usually doing our homework when the sun set; my mother would call us to the window to watch the sky change colors. The homework could wait; nature would not.

During the winter when we looked outside and saw the last bits of sunlight fall on the frozen snow, everything looked placid, immobile—uneventful. Invariably, one of us would comment to my mother that there is nothing happening out there, everything is so still. No matter how still and/or insignificant everything seemed, nature was at work, as usual. Winter is a special kind of work.

Deliberate stillness is winter's motive. While nothing in nature is forced before its time, nature uses the power of cold and ice—elements evident in change—to force us to be still so we can remember, restore, and resume. It takes strong acts to make humans still. Nature uses the might of winter to stop us so we are forced to find gentleness. Scorned by many, with its barren, intimidating pose, winter is actually a most supportive season that uses vigor to gently lead us inward, to find strength that will take us outward to inevitably meet spring.

Bringing barrenness and sharp air, winter's dark cloak is dreaded. But the solemn garment winter wears is but a shield disguising its warm essence. With its shadowed afternoons and bright black nights, winter sheds a great light and stirs a deep warmth. These are found as human beings are drawn within, where, in an atmosphere of personal silence, we enter interior worlds. In the depths of winter, forward movement continues as inner exploration begins.

Darkness casts its own light as wintertimes of change offer the broadest reach of inner light. This is a light of memory, reflecting understanding and meaning that winter darkness brings into view. Inner light penetrates as it reaches through layers of human coverings to discover what lies beneath the surface. Dark periods of change ignite this light that takes us underneath where

There is one glory of the sun, and another of the moon, and another glory of the stars: for one star differeth from another star in glory.

1 CORINTHIANS
15:41 (KJV)

possibilities for growth lie quietly still, but breathing.

Though loss is peculiar and challenging, it is the catalyst for going deeper into oneself. There we mine for treasured remembrances that inner light reveals. Without loss, and sometimes dramatic change, there is often no reason to cast this light and hold it up to the past. But with forward movement at a slower pace, coupled with feelings of vulnerability loss and change bring, timing is ideal to go underneath the surface to search for hidden strength.

Growth is produced not only by looking ahead, but also by looking back to contemplate previous progress. Winter is the time to look back and remember, to take stock. In winter, quietude and introspection are available. Here we are encouraged to find the essence of yesterday to take with us into tomorrow.

Even though onyxed spells of melancholy cast shadows over future suns, a light shines throughout the bleak days of transition. Transition to tomorrow is supported by stars of memory shining against a dark sky of loss. Using our inner light to discover memories, yesterday's essence is captured as tomorrow's strength is claimed. Underneath still surfaces live the echoes of yesterday and the whispers of tomorrow. The heart

He who has no time to mourn has no time to mend.

JOHN DONNE

hears them all. In winters of change, we are stilled and given the chance to hear them too.

The Heart's Coves

At the end of the movie *The Wizard of Oz*, the wizard gives the tin man a heart to make him complete. The wizard tells the tin man, "And remember, my sentimental friend, hearts will never be made practical until they are made unbreakable."

Unbreakable hearts. Impossible. They are just not made that way. When we choose to live fully and participate in the life experience, hearts are open and, therefore, exposed to all sorts of elements. They meet the hope of spring, the warmth of summer, the chill of autumn, and the darkness of winter. As our hearts expose themselves, they capture all that is being recorded while we are busy living the seasons of our lives.

This recording is made up of memories stored in coves in the heart. Here, in recessed chambers, live experiences of every kind. Yesterdays company together, sharing similarities, revealing differences. Some memories have been favored, forgotten, or abandoned. While memories differ in their composition, they all have one thing in common: they are alive. These remembrances, archived for the future, are referred to as change prompts us to visit them now.

Keep thy heart with all diligence; for out of it are the issues of life.

PROVERBS 4:23 (KJV)

When we go out and live our lives, we tend to forge ahead and can miss the messages of our todays with our eyes and actions fixed on the future. The heart misses nothing. As we slow down to sort through our state of goodbye, yesterday's messages have a chance to be heard and seen. Though initially blurry and the full value of them hard to see, now is a time to look to the heart, remember and recognize the past, and let ourselves feel yesterday's strength.

The heart defines an individual. It is the core of one's being, the essence of oneself. Though hearts bear within their coves the majesties and malices of yesterday, the memories they capture are the foundation on which tomorrow is built. What we have done, what has been done for us, and what remains undone, all remind us to look to the heart to tell us what we accomplished in our past. This offers insight and courage for what we can accomplish in the present and future.

Our memories are the bits of fortitude we need to help us carry on. Reminders of days well spent, of words honestly spoken, of eyes that held truth, serve as fortification. This is the nectar of yesterday. When time moves on, as it must, the nectar is what we take with us to remind ourselves of what has been, to help us believe in what is yet to be.

Although the world is full of suffering, it is full also of the overcoming of it.

HELEN KELLER

Advancement, whether an infinitesimal step or a gigantic leap, is a measure of growth that occurs to bring us to where we are. These are cubits of confidence gained. When we remember what we have done, we are reminded of what we can do. We do not wither unless we choose to. Though loss will come and weaken strength, we are defeated only when we succumb to what is about us rather than remembering what is within us.

We know life will never be without loss. Never. Announcing itself subtly or abruptly, it will come. But our ability to cope and make a transition cannot be blamed on someone or something else, even if loss is another's fault. When the imposition of loss is a deliberate act caused by someone or something else, adjustment to it remains our responsibility. This can be a hard choice to make. Knowing that someone else is the reason for our pain makes greater the challenge to cope with loss. Nevertheless, this fact remains: the outcome of the future lies solely with us.

A choice made to adjust to loss and go through the tunnel toward the light is supported in part by the way memories are brought out of their coves and interpreted. The interpretation of the past, such as recognition of its invaluable teachings and its wisdom for living future days, determines the extent to which spring will be met and most fully lived. By identifying and understanding

Great thoughts always come from the heart.

FRENCH PROVERB

what we gained from yesterday, we can gain some sustenance to meet what lies ahead. Using the heart's recollections to best advantage enables us to come out into the light of spring with a ray of hope.

Winter's white veil is the covering behind which strength for spring lies. Lifting of the veil comes not from spring but from a personal decision to search for the strength which yesterday held. Rich discoveries await those who journey into the coves of the heart where yesterdays live. And while attentive to other matters, interior matters, morning light begins to arrive earlier as evening light lingers. Spring nears. The journey inward advances the journey outward. Winter darkness proves preparatory. It is the bridge connected to spring. Having spent time in our own light, we are ready to walk across this bridge to meet the hope that waits to meet us.

For where your treasure is, there will your heart be also.

MATTHEW 6:21 (KJV)

Winter Exercises

WINTER IMAGE TRIGGERS	Add Your List Here
fireplaces	_____
shovels	_____
hot soup	_____
frozen streams	_____
snowstorms	_____
beef stew	_____
poinsettias	_____
Christmas	_____
boots	_____
ice	_____
Hanukkah	_____
snowmobiling	_____
hockey	_____
skiing	_____
snow days	_____
ice fishing	_____
hot chocolate	_____
wool sweaters	_____
roasting marshmallows	_____
cookies and milk for Santa	_____
parkas	_____
snow angels	_____
pine cones	_____
sleds	_____
mittens	_____

WINTER MEMORIES

When we are going through change from a loss, we become very sensitive to images and sounds. Everything, it seems, is a reminder. Looking at photographs and listening to music are among the most memory-provoking of stimuli.

PHOTOGRAPHS

There are many things that stir our memories when we are going through change. Among them are special photographs. Look at some photographs that are meaningful to you. If there are people in the pictures, what are the faces saying? The eyes? Write the words they are speaking to you. Write the words you remember exchanging with the person(s) in the photographs that day. If certain photographs of objects or scenery trigger emotion, write what your heart remembers about them. Take as long as you need to look at photographs, and as much time as you want to write about them. Return to this exercise whenever you like. Memories aren't only good to recall in wintertimes of change, but throughout our lives, whenever we have the need to touch part of our past.

MUSIC

Have you ever noticed how a certain song can take you right back to a place in your history? The sound of a familiar melody or the lyrics of a song can place us at a point in time we relive through memory. Listening to music that is special, favored, and relative to a significant time you experienced can bring memories to the fore. Choose some music that evokes special memories, and listen to it. Then write down where you were and with whom, if anyone, when you first heard this music.

Describe the setting. How did the music make you feel then? How does it make you feel now?

CLUSTERING

There is a writing practice known as clustering, or webbing, that helps writers brainstorm on paper. It lets ideas freely flow from the brain in a nonlinear stream. It is easy to do. Your journal may not be roomy enough for clustering. Try it there, but you can also use large pieces of paper for clustering, at least 8 1/2" x 11" sheets of paper. And save your clusters! There are stories, memories, and insights in those free-floating words.

Put a word or phrase in the center of the paper. Make this word or phrase the name of a person related to the loss in your life. Circle it. Draw lines from the center circle and connect empty circles to them. Fill the circles in with words or phrases the central word brings to mind. Keep adding on as you think of new words or ideas that are prompted from the central word. Keep going. Let the circles continue to branch out. When you come to the point when you have filled in a page, go to your journal and write out those connections and what they mean to you. There is a story in them. What is it saying to you?

Don't try to understand your cluster while you are creating it. Don't stop to analyze it. In Gabriele Lusser Rico's book *Writing the Natural Way* (which thoroughly explains clustering), she tells readers to "simply relax and doodle, letting the circles and lines shape a pleasing pattern. That very nonlinear act will break down your resistance and you will find yourself filling in those inviting empty circles with the associations that are inevitably triggered by the nucleus word."

Another way to do clustering is to take a phrase or word from the "Catching Phrases" exercise (discussed further on) and use it in your center circle. Or, take a word from the seasonal "Image Triggers." You can cluster in any season, at any time. It is a way to let yourself see on paper how wide your thoughts and emotions flow in your brain and help you understand yourself and your change.

Below is an example of a cluster I did, followed by my written interpretation of it.

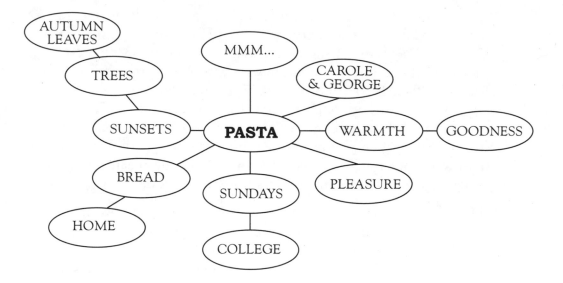

Pasta. Such a happy food. No matter the weather, the season, it is always welcome, for it always welcomes. I like pasta. No, I love it! It makes me feel warmed, like I so often felt when I was at Carole and George's house.

It's no longer Carole and George. Change came. Yet, with all that change took, it left to me my memories—memories of Carole and George and how moments with them made me feel. Sitting in that room with all those windows, watching the sunset on autumn afternoons. It was good. And when I smell pasta and taste its softness, I am warmed. I am reminded of how much I was loved then, and how much I still am now. Nothing could change the love.

DIALOGUE WITH CLOTHING—AGAIN

Just as clothing was used to explain its memory of a loss, clothing can be used to describe its memories of special events it experienced. Let your clothing have life. Let it use its memory to record what it saw and felt yesterday. Resist the temptation to think for the clothing; let it think. Get out of the way mentally so you can give the sweater, gloves, uniform, etc. the room it needs to voice itself.

CATCHING PHRASES

Sometimes when we are reading we come across a particular phrase, or one word, that captures our attention. It may be the sound of the phrase we like. Or, it may hit us because it strikes a nerve. Write down a phrase that is meaningful to you. It might be a line from a favorite poem, a phrase in a book or newspaper, or a passage from the Bible or Talmud. Maybe a phrase or quote from this book stirs you.

Go to your journal and write down the phrase or word at the top of a blank page. Write it slowly. Think about the word. Write it again. Then, begin to write about what the word or phrase is saying to you. Why is it special? What does it make you think of? Remember? How does it make you feel? Why do you think you are drawn to it? Write what its message is personally delivering to you.

CHAPTER 5

Spring

Mourning to Morning

Spring sun ascends
   Hope
is raised.

New rains fall
   Cleansing
showers the earth.

Tender buds bask
   Growth
Beginnings have begun.

When milder breezes replace bitter winds, forsythias stretch their limbs, and crocuses peer up from the ground, signs are clear winter has passed. It feels safe to go out. Freedom stirs.

Delicate buds tightly holding tender petals together gradually—ever so gradually—move above the earth, beyond the branch, looking for warm winds to trust. Gingerly, nature releases buds from their coil and they yield to the warming trend of spring. Gardens become quietly active as bright colors begin appearing on land ready for growth. There is a sense of belief rising. Renewal stems.

As spring arrives with its gentle and inviting features, a sense of trust encourages growth. Growth can be cautiously approached after a significant goodbye. But spring's invitation welcomes. It ushers in a host of textures, fragrances, and colors that stimulate the senses. Something new is ahead. With the pivotal point of change seasons away from us, and winter introspection behind us, insights are gained, memories' essences are secured, and a rekindled desire to meet life begins to grow. Spring's invitation to come outside is appealing.

To come to the spring season after loss is to come to hope. The cycle, thus far, has brought new meaning and wisdom. With these in place, hope

In season,
all is good.

SOPHOCLES

is raised anew. It is now possible to begin fresh, or continue—to move ahead to find new meaning in life. Hurts can heal. Clear spring skies energize interest and promote wonder in outer activity. We move beyond introspection. With healing in process, we step outside ourselves to see what is beginning to grow, to see what waits to be discovered.

Healing takes place when we realize that, even though something significant in life is lost, life still goes on and continues to offer import and intrigue for us to explore. When we reach this point in the process of goodbye, we reach out to the future with one hand and let go of the past with the other. We are open. We are well on the way to hello when we glimpse a glimmer of the future and wish to bring into view a broader vision of its possibilities.

In an effort to make that view as wide and as engaging as it can be, the final frost is to be met. Here the past is considered and final impediments are cleared to make free the path of spring, so future hope can prevail.

Saying Goodbye: A Choice

A final north wind brings with it a gallant reminder of what has been and heralds a plea: release the past. Even though spring has arrived, mourning lingers for what has been. In an effort

We are healed of a suffering only by experiencing it to the full.

Marcel Proust

to go from mourning to morning, two things have to take place. First, the past is to be upheld for what it was. And then, to ensure hope is not overshadowed by yesterday's presence, the past must be let go. It is time to say goodbye.

Saying goodbye is a choice. If we choose not to say goodbye, we are bound by a pain that harnesses the procession of life. You may have heard it said, "No decision is a decision." After a painful goodbye we can expect to hurt for a while. But, eventually, a time comes when we want to be free from pain. If that timing is postponed, we either are not ready to say goodbye or we are not willing to do so. Unwillingness is a decision that rests with each of us.

We have more control over and responsibility for the outcome of situations in our lives than we would like to admit. Pain, particularly when it is deep, especially when it is a deliberate act by someone else, gives us a seemingly good reason to hold on to the past. It wasn't our fault. "He died"; "she left"; "they did it," are the emphatic cries of those who hurt, many of which are valid.

However, the responsibility to react to such cries does not belong to others. It belongs to us. Indeed, we may want someone who has hurt us to make it better by undoing what they have done. "Why did they have to die?" "Why did we move?" "Why did the relationship end?" This

Destiny is not a matter of chance; it is a matter of choice.

WILLIAM JENNINGS BRYAN

kind of question can haunt us for so long that we may miss the joys of life. To strain over "what was" or "what might have been" takes precious time away from us. Life, in its fleeting fashion, could be better spent looking at and enjoying what is before us than pondering what is behind us, a yesterday we cannot change.

Some goodbyes inflict deep hurt. Relief from such pain comes not when we deny a loss but when we accept it and say goodbye. It takes courage to admit that something happened, had penetrating effects, and is now over. Choosing to do this indicates a willingness to move forward, whatever the future holds. Spring holds an element of freedom that gives us the courage to say what needs to be said to ourselves and to others, to move in a forward direction.

Expressing Goodbye

To say goodbye to the past is to acknowledge it for all its truths. This can be done in various ways. Write in your journal. This is an important way to visit yesterday's experiences and address them; let them speak to you. Speak with someone who is objective about your goodbye. Express your thoughts and feelings verbally with someone from the ministerial community or a professional counselor. Individuals unrelated to the experience can offer a safe place where

Growth consists of long involved processes.

JOSEPH GIRZONE

objectivity and openness are available and where goodbye can be met successfully.

In addition to speaking with objective parties, speaking with those involved with a goodbye offers assistance. Also, joining support groups can help. To face people, along with facing feelings, is a true challenge. When the challenge is met, it breeds confidence.

Writing Letters

Along with physically meeting with people to express our feelings, letter-writing is a powerful means of closure. Closure, the goal of goodbye, allows us to close on the past and open to the future. Writing letters is one of the most effective ways to say goodbye.

When you write a letter you have the opportunity to privately and thoughtfully express your feelings. They are given a place. Similar to the practice of keeping a journal, writing a letter enables you to validate what you feel by giving your emotions substance by the use of words. When you write specifically "to" the person or place or experience that held loss for you, you are telling them, and yourself, that what you went through was real and they were a part of it.

Furthermore, when you "speak" to someone in writing, you maintain the floor. It is a one-sided conversation where no interruptions are allowed.

Ordinarily in letters we do not ramble on and on, as we can in speech. We choose our words more carefully, even in informal letters, and give thought to what we will or will not include.

THOMAS MOORE

There are no protests or arguments. Your written articulation of feelings is likely to be fluid as you name your audience and keep them foremost in your mind.

This experience can feel foreign if you have never done it before. Just chalk it up to everything else that feels unusual during a changeful goodbye. If writing a letter helps, if it makes the difference between looking back less frequently and looking ahead more often and more hopefully, do it. Any discomfort letter-writing stirs will wane once its therapeutic properties take effect.

After you sit down and write your letter, you may wonder about sending it. It takes more courage to share a letter than it does to write one. Consider this: Whether or not you decide to send the letter to the addressee (if this is possible) isn't as important as actually writing it. When you literally spell out your feelings, you have, in essence, taken the opportunity to tell someone how you feel and why. Shredding or sharing your letter will not dilute its efficacy. Healing and closure will be assisted and sealed, whether a letter is saved, sent, or destroyed.

If you decide to send the letter, you should be aware that the recipient will be filled with emotions that you may be asked to address. The recipient has emotional needs too. Their reaction to your letter may trigger a need to put closure

The past is gone; the future will never be: Now we are under Grace.

JOEL GOLDSMITH

on their side of the situation. A letter intended for your closure given to someone else may require interaction with the recipient, which may or may not be appropriate. When someone opens your letter, you are opening their heart and mind and inciting their emotions. This may lead them to turn to you for their own closure. Therefore, be prepared for possible future contact. If this is something you are opposed to or unprepared for, do not send the letter. (Specific exercises on letter-writing are explained at the end of this chapter.)

Other Letters

Writing letters can be useful in other forms too. For example, you might want to write to family members and friends who are not the reason for a change and tell them how you feel about a goodbye you (or both of you) are going through. This helps us understand one another better. As you know, emotions shift after a loss, and even though people know us well, after a loss we do not know ourselves at times, and those we know may need some help recognizing us. Also, the people who know us might be able to help us better understand ourselves during this time.

Open and honest communication is essential if we are to have rich and mutually supportive relationships. Such communication is paramount when we live through goodbyes. There is a

Some try to keep a tangible reminder:
a flower,
a photograph,
a handkerchief,
perhaps. A writer tries to preserve it in words.

ARTHUR GORDON

tendency, however, to take the people in closest proximity to us for granted. It is astounding how many relationships are lived out side by side where an understanding of what another is feeling is presumed rather than learned. There can be miles between the hearts of those living in the same house when communication is unclear or silent, and yet no emotional distance at all between friends who are separated by a state, a nation, or a continent if they take the time to articulate the events of their lives and put their thoughts and feelings in writing.

Just because people live with us or near us does not mean they know what is going on inside of us. Yes, actions do speak loudly, but not always as clearly as words. Use them. It does not take many words to let someone close to us know what we are feeling and why so that they can be close to us, not just physically but emotionally. When we achieve emotional closeness it matters not where someone is physically, because we always feel them near.

Close relationships have the potential to become stronger as communication becomes clearer. Bonds tighten when a woman writes a letter to her husband after her mother's death; or when a father writes to his son after a divorce; or when a sister who lives just around the corner writes to her sister after a miscarriage. We give time and

To thine own self be true, then thou cannot be false to any man.

WILLIAM SHAKESPEARE

attention to relationships when we place importance on feelings and their expression. Very often some of the most wonderful beginnings occur within long-standing relationships when changeful goodbyes are addressed. Friendships and family ties can be rejuvenated and fortified as a deeper unity is fostered by way of open communication. This unity assists healing and makes bonds stronger. It leads us forward.

Communication clarifies our feelings and frees us. Self-expression comes in many forms, and letter-writing, among the most beneficial and progressive, is but one way to honestly and clearly communicate. Whatever way we choose to comfortably and effectively wash away residual pain, that way must be utilized and respected if we are to be free of emotional impairments. Such freedom enables the breadth of the future to envelop us.

❦

In the spring of change we are again a tenderfoot. We have been at beginnings before, but not this one. Each stirring of newness that quivers in every spring is one met fresh. When the land shepherds seeds to rise and bloom, we are encouraged by these sprouts, and we want to believe we can rise too. We can. To give in to hope and want to be gifted by life once again is to be certain that we will be.

Everybody needs beauty as well as bread, places to play in and pray in, where Nature may heal and cheer and give strength to body and soul alike.

JOHN MUIR

Spring Exercises

SPRING IMAGE TRIGGERS	*Add Your List Here*
bicycles	_____
baseball	_____
daffodils	_____
tennis	_____
green lawns	_____
March Madness	_____
lilacs	_____
Passover	_____
yo-yos	_____
cotton jackets	_____
Frisbees	_____
Easter	_____
crocuses	_____
birds chirping	_____
fertilizer	_____
softball	_____
jump ropes	_____
open windows with screens	_____
walking in the rain	_____
morning dew	_____
badminton	_____
Sunday drives	_____
hopscotch	_____
dyeing Easter eggs	_____

WRITING LETTERS

Write a letter to someone or something no longer in your life as before. The change in your life may include a goodbye to a loved one, a house, a career. Write a letter telling the person, place, or thing what you are feeling. Tell them what is on your heart. Do this exercise when you are ready.

In this letter, as you feel led, express any of the following:

✝ The highlight of your relationship with the person or object.

  Specifically tell what it was about them that enhanced your life because of your relationship together.

✝ The most disappointing experience you remember.

  What happened in the relationship that disappointed you? Was it the way it ended? Was it something that was done or left undone? Express your disappointment and anger here. Explain why you were hurt. Be clear and be honest.

✝ Do you have any regrets about the relationship?

  What do you regret? Why do you think something was not said or done? Did you do or say something you wish you had not? Wish they had not? What was it? Write it out.

✝ Say goodbye.

  Did you actually say goodbye to the person, place, or object? If you did not, if you did not have the chance or the courage, now is a chance. Perhaps now you have the courage. If not, read on, carry on. Your time to say goodbye will come.

OTHER LETTERS

Write a letter to the person/people you live with or near. Tell your wife, husband, son, daughter, parent, friend what you are feeling as a result of your change. Don't assume they know. Tell them what you have come to know based on your reactions to events that have changed your life, or theirs. Make the letter as short or long as you like. Put it in an envelope, seal it, and deliver it to them personally. Invite them to read it privately. This is an act of courage. This is an act of love. Be brave.

WRITE A LETTER TO YOURSELF

Write a letter to yourself. Start it off with Dear [your name]. In this letter, tell yourself what you are feeling as a result of your loss, and why. Explain as many of the details as you can. Don't stop to defend, analyze, or reduce your feelings. Just write them straight from your heart. Make the letter as long as it should be.

After you have written the letter, put it in an envelope, seal it, and put it away somewhere for safe keeping. Open this letter in six months. Put a note on your calendar to remind you. Six months later, read the letter and let it reveal to you where you have emotionally traveled since then. How have you progressed? What is most striking about the difference between your feelings then and now? Is there a contrast? In what ways are you relieved you are six months away from where you were?

Answer these questions in your journal, and any others that come to mind. Explore in writing where you have been and where you are now.

FIRST TIMES

PART I

The "first times" in our lives are those new activities that blossomed into a garden of experience. They created our histories. Do you remember the first time you:

drove a car	stayed up all night at a slumber party
flew on a plane	stayed up all night to study
went to school	bought your first house
went back to school	sold your first car
watched your child go to school	received an allowance
cashed a paycheck	spent an allowance
wrote a check	dated
wrote a love letter	rode a bicycle
took a vacation	rode a horse
gave blood	kissed that special person
gave birth	had a pet
went to work	had a root canal
went to college	had no curfew
made dinner	grew a garden
burned dinner	lived a dream

Add to this list, and think about your first times. Think with your pen in your hand while visiting your journal. Consider your firsts and let details of beginnings germane to your life lead you to write about where you have traveled since then; how you, only you, could arrive to this point in your life because of the firsts you have lived. They are your unique firsts, never experienced by another. Explore them. Take as much time as each "first" requires.

PART II

Spring is the time for more firsts. Think about the first times you are pondering or have experienced since the pivotal point of change in your life; for example, walking into a room or a favorite restaurant without meeting the sting of loss; touching, or even seeing your toes again after a pregnancy; really enjoying a day of retirement.

What firsts hold special meaning now? Is there a first you anticipate experiencing that will make you feel better, more confident, happy, encouraged? Write about these firsts. Our gardens of experience continue to grow in us, as long as we let them. Let them. And, in the meantime, tend to the meaning of these firsts in your journal. Weed through your thoughts and feelings. Watch what continues to grow.

CHAPTER 6

Summer

A New Sun

Over bridges of time
 eastern skies cross
Dawning on sunsets.
 Yesterday was.

 Today is.

Full meaning blooms
 inviting participation
 Life glows.
New castles are built
 on the shores of acceptance.
 Yesterday was.

 Today is.

Azure skies watch over dawns lush with pos-sibilities. Blades of grass, softened and strengthened by time, pliantly erect themselves from a foundation once frozen to an earthly altar that awaited their arrival with patience. This summer sky, a promising canvas, is a welcome blue expanse eyes willingly open to, eager to see what the longest awaited light in the seasons of change has to reveal.

In the fullness of beauty and hope, summer stands. Growth undenied, rejoices. Encouraged and nurtured by darkness, cold, moisture, sunlight, and warmth, summer spreads itself wide in tantalizing aromas, textures, and sights that invite all to this celebration of life. The reach of summer extends as near as one's backyard or to a mountain peak a continent away. Its depth of purpose takes each person to the height of summertime's goal: participation in life.

In spring we see possibilities. In summer we believe in them. A new sun, the brightest sun, gives rise to new reaches of hope we no longer view from a distance but touch as we feel part of reality again. Discoveries abound. By choosing to seek, in the summer of change, we find.

Summer culminates the cycle of change. To meet this point is to withdraw from ourselves and reach outside to engage in life and become fully involved in all that is. Goodbyes lead to

One can enjoy a rainbow without necessarily forgetting the forces that made it.

MARK TWAIN

emotional shifts, e.g., denial, anger, sorrow, interior introspection where memories and meanings are gleaned, to closure and renewed hope, and finally to acceptance. When loss has gone full circle, we arrive in summer, completing the journey through goodbye.

Understanding comes by summer's light. It is the light of wisdom. By this sun, strength shines, penetrating hearts that are ready to meet truth. This readiness has come gradually, seen only in seconds at first, then into long hours of peace and strength. Understanding comes when we are ready for it and not before. In summer we are ready. We come to the peace we need because we come to accept.

To arrive at summer and glory in its fullness is to arrive at acceptance. Acceptance does not necessarily mean agreement with what changed in our lives, but it does mean the resulting effects have been acknowledged, processed, and accepted. To accept is to know peace, a peace that settles within which rests on a decision to be open to truth. Acceptance comes when a goodbye has been lived through—cried through, remembered through, cursed through, or written through. There is a readiness for life, a desire to meet it head on once again. Effects of goodbye no longer hinder us from immersing ourselves in the here

The great thing in this world is not so much where we stand, but in what direction we are moving.

OLIVER WENDELL HOLMES

and now. Yesterday is past; its essence remains. Today is here, and so are we.

Being here, fully present to experience life, is to open up the senses, air them out, and let them be stimulated by all that is flourishing around us. Belief and belonging are the gifts of summer. To receive them is to simply be open to them. In this warmest time of the year, unnecessary layers of clothing, emotions—coverings—are shed. Free of encumbrances, we are free to live. To embrace such freedom is to allow oneself to be embraced by it. Summer's ability to touch us is in proportion to our willingness to be touched by it. This occurs when we accept what has been.

Drawn into summer's bounty, we find new discoveries among what once appeared common to us, or what we took for granted summers ago. We follow whatever soothes the senses and heightens the soul. Having gone through loss, summer offers a fullness unfelt in previous seasons. It has much to give, and we are ready to receive.

The soul, open to sensory stimulation because of its need for variety, is stirred by what is near it. When we reach a summertime state of heart there is conscious desire for stimulation, a desire to receive the richness of summer's offerings.

The further removed we are emotionally from loss, the better the opportunity will be to remember it

There is a time for departure even when there's no certain place to go.

TENNESSEE WILLIAMS

The soul doesn't have to know what is going on in life. It doesn't need interpretations, explanations, or conclusions, but it does require musing, reverie, consideration, wonder, and exploration.

THOMAS MOORE

differently. In summer we do just that. We look back, but not for long. And when we do, it no longer has the effect it once did. Let me give you a very simple illustration.

Christmas is my favorite time of year. I have loved this season since I was a child. Its beauty, meaning, and embodiment of spirituality captivate me, year after year. Given my affection for the season, when it is time to take the Christmas tree down and put the decorations in the basement, I am melancholy that day and usually for a few days following. I must get accustomed to the "barrenness" of my home and reacquaint myself with its familiarity minus Christmas ornamentation.

When I clean up after the holidays and vacuum the living room, I am saddened by the sight of lingering pine needles. I'm too close to the event to feel differently. But, when I vacuum in July and discover a few stray pine needles under the sofa, I am not sad. In truth, I am delighted. It is a glad sight to find remnants of Christmas on a steamy summer afternoon. I can look at them and be joyful without feeling the gloom I did when I discovered them soon after they fell.

Distance between events brings decreased emotional intensity and effects. As time passes, and if it is used well, distance serves to support our transition in a healthy fashion. The more time passes from an event and the more we have sought to go through painful change and wrestle with it, the more apt we are to meet it in memory without its having an emotive claim on us.

Now that we have come to accept what the past has brought, various sights, sounds, etc. that we encounter will evoke memories but won't leave us diminished by them. Having come further along in the cycle of change, we are ready to meet life. We expect it to remind us of yesterday, but we do not let ourselves stay there and risk missing the experience and memory-making of today. Reactions to life's gifts are bound to bring us back to what has been. But these reactions no longer have the power they once had. Reduced and put into appropriate perspective, emotions and various memories are places we visit but are no longer places we stay.

Casting itself in subtle or vibrant shades of promise, summer convinces us to believe in today and every today to come. The summer sun sets on the past and rises on the future. Its beauty—radiant, serene, compelling—reflects a magnificence we help to define. Summer's fullness and belief in life and all it can be is completed by what we contribute to it. This is a contribution a cycle of change seems to diminish but, in fact, replenishes.

Glistening on the truth that steady efforts bring forth fruit and that the purpose of goodbye is for

When these memories knock at the door of our consciousness we open the door to see who is there and we acknowledge them. But we do not invite them in to spend the entire day with us.

JOYCE RUPP

a beginning, our spirits are richly filled with power and purpose. The harmony of these truths plays a familiar melody. We know it. It is the harmony of the spirit inside us. It is the one we know best. Melodies differ from person to person, for we are composed of various notes. While we differ in composition, an orchestra is at work. A human symphony is being conducted concurrently on small and large scales.

In summertime we rediscover our place in the symphony, behold it, and know it is meaningful. When we fall into summer's embrace and accept goodbye for all it was and was not, we hear our melody again and are ready to take our place, knowing we have a contribution to make and what we have to offer makes a difference.

Under the summer sun the present and future live. Here life basks. This sun, reflecting warm rays of ease, peace, and anticipation, shines on the faces of those whose eyes now look upward with belief. Yesterday was. Today is. We are.

Spirit is an invisible force made visible in all life.

Maya Angelou

Summer Exercises

SUMMER IMAGE TRIGGERS   *Add Your List Here*

honeysuckle   _____
watermelon   _____
cotton candy   _____
Independence Day   _____
strawberry picking   _____
sailing   _____
iced tea   _____
thunderstorms   _____
seashore   _____
bare feet   _____
geraniums   _____
summer stock plays   _____
sandcastles   _____
mountains   _____
ice cream cones   _____
vacation   _____
barbecues   _____
catching fireflies   _____
campsites   _____
poison ivy   _____
jellyfish   _____
corn on the cob   _____
sunburn   _____

SENSE-ABILITIES

One day, I was in the supermarket to pick up basil I needed for a recipe I was making. When I didn't see any, I asked the man in produce if the store was out of it. He told me there was a fresh supply that hadn't been put out yet. He went to get it.

When he came back with the wooden carton, he began opening it up and then suddenly stopped what he was doing. He told me that the aroma of the basil brought him right back to his childhood. He had lived in a house where he and his parents lived upstairs and his grandparents downstairs. They gardened. They grew fresh basil. The fragrance of the basil made him think of when he was a little boy and he would wake up on summer mornings and smell the fragrance coming through his bedroom window. I listened to the brief account and watched his face and eyes, and I knew that in these moments he was far from that supermarket. He was in yesterday. He was in that house. And, clearly, he was delighted to be there.

Where do you go when certain fragrances, sights, and sounds touch you? Follow them. Follow the images that come to mind when you eat a certain food, smell a particular fragrance, see a familiar sight. Live the moment. Give yourself time to let your mind go where your senses take you. Then go to your journal and write about your thoughts and feelings. Take as much time as you need to follow as many thoughts as your senses lead you to follow. It is likely these mental travels will come up unexpectedly, so have your journal handy so you can write while it is all fresh in your mind. It will be exciting to see where your thoughts lead you.

GOING OUTSIDE

Stop. Take time to look at what nature is revealing to you. Summer is the time to go outside. Go. Stare at the sky at different times during the day. Get up early and watch the sun rise. Watch it set. Go outside of your home at night and look at the sky and the stars; go to the park and watch the birds, the trees. Don't just glance. Look. Listen. Let your senses respond and guide you. Bring your journal along and jot down what your senses are keen to. Don't ignore different longings. Follow them. Go outside, and outside of yourself.

ANSWERS TO CONSIDER

Below is a series of questions. Ponder the answers to them in your journal. Take them, one at a time, whenever you feel like dwelling on one of them. Remember, in journal writing there are no right or wrong answers—there are only "your" answers.

✝   What is your fondest memory about the person, place, or thing you are missing?

✝   What is your most unpleasant memory?

✝   What do you think you lost the most by losing a loved one, object, experience, etc.?

✝   What do you think you gained the most by having the experience with that special person, place, or thing?

✝   What is your deepest regret regarding the loss in your life? Why?

✝ How will you look at your life and use the time ahead to ease regret in the future?

✝ Physically, where do you feel the most fear?

✝ Emotionally, where do you feel the most fear?

✝ If you had the courage to say whatever you wanted to someone, to whom would you say it and what would you say?

✝ Write about someone you admire, preferably someone with whom you have personal contact, not necessarily an individual of fame or celebrity. If you could extract some of their character and add it to your own, what would you take? What would you use it for?

✝ If you could do anything you wanted to do, what would it be? Why would you choose to do this?

✝ Have you told the people in your life (the ones in the best of health, the weak, the successful, the challenged) what they mean to you and why? Why or why not? Do you plan to tell them? When?

✝ Have you told yourself what you mean to yourself and why?

THINKING AHEAD

Consider things in life you have always wanted to do. They may be things you put aside and chalked up to fanciful thinking and then quickly abandoned for what you believed to be "more important." Now is the time to get reacquainted with possibilities you entertained.

Do you have a special travel interest, a place you have wanted to visit, a friend or relative you have considered going to visit? Or, perhaps you want to engage in a sport you have never tried, become a gourmet cook (or just a cook), learn a musical instrument, plant a garden, or paint. Maybe you would like to spend some time cultivating a new relationship or weeding out an existing one to make the ground more fertile for better experiences to grow. There are interests and considerations that stimulate us at different times for various reasons, and we tend to put them off to "one day." One day is here.

It is not true that we don't have time for someone or something. It is true that we don't make time for someone or something. We can find time for what is important to us. When you decide to spend yourself on something, to engage in a new activity, you are not only giving time to the activity but in essence to yourself.

You are showing you care about you. Do you remember in the "Beginnings" chapter I wrote that you are going to your journal but you are really going to yourself? Well, it is no different when you engage in something you desire to invest your time in. You may go to a musical instrument, a golf lesson, your kitchen, a friend, or a park, but you are really going to yourself. When we give ourselves the people, places, or things we need, we are fulfilling whatever it is we need within, and, in so doing, come to have that much more to give to everyone and everything we are connected to.

Write about the things you would like to do with time ahead. Your ideas can be as short or as long as you like. Then, write the answer to "Why" you want to do something. Take each item one by one. Give it thought. Give it time.

After you have written the answer to "Why," write the answer to "How." Carefully consider small steps you could take to begin something new. It may be as simple as a phone call to someone you know is already doing the thing you want to do. Or, it could be a call to a school or organization that might send you a brochure on that course you want to take or the group you want to join. Whatever it is, it has already begun, because the thought is alive. Consider what you can do in writing to make it happen; then, carry out what you have written and watch it happen.

CHAPTER 7

Reprise

Autumn change, winter remembrance, spring hope, summer fullness. The seasons change, and we within them, as we live through the goodbyes of our lives. Following its cyclical pattern, the seasons turn around and around. Like ocean waves spilling onto the shore, seasonal turns are consistent, yet consistently different. As they arrive and depart with a natural evenness, the seasons flow familiarly but never present the same offerings. Their timing is perfect, their purposes unique. As the seasons unfold, they reveal their features and fulfill their purposes. In the process, they teach us we are meant to do the same.

Nature embarks on a relentless quest for growth. As it changes, nature repeatedly demonstrates that growth requires release and connection, confusion and clarity, darkness and brightness, bitterness and warmth. As these polars respectively align, they gradually support fusions that reveal purposes and engender understanding. No matter how strong the winds, how torrential the rains, how penetrating the sun, growth is the goal.

When it comes time for the seasons to change, one does not eclipse the other. Each season supports the next one's arrival. There is no hierarchy. They are equal. Each is necessary. With no bests, no betters, one season is not revered above another. This is as it should be. For without the strength, defined character, and support of the

Nature does not proceed by leaps and bounds.

LINNAEUS

preceding season, not one could arrive, give, and fulfill its purpose. This truth is no different for humans.

There is meaning in each season of the year, each season of change we live through. As hard as it is to make transitions and to let go of familiar sights, sounds, and textures, we are to release our grasp. This surrender enables the supporting elements of life to keep us moving forward to a new series of purposes to be fulfilled. Each season follows the next; each season moves forward. For as long as we are given breath, we, too, are meant to move forward, in natural evolution, fulfilling the purpose of our lives.

And what is our purpose? It can seem worthless, or at best small, when we face a challenging goodbye that leaves us uncertain. It may appear that we have little to contribute to the whole. Still, our presence is purposeful. We were given life for a reason. Each one who touches this soil, for however long or brief, has a destiny to fulfill. Our reason for being may not be understood or clearly seen, especially when we struggle to advance through goodbye. But advancement is in process as long as we keep an eye to the future and an eye to the heart. This perspective leads us with a vision far clearer than our mental view alone.

What we give to others, we give to ourselves.

Marianne Williamson

Our purpose is to grow into the strongest person we can be, to give our individual offerings to the world. No matter what our private world consists of, however small or large its scope, we are to heal ourselves from the results of loss. As we do this, we are able to continue to contribute to our personal worlds, thus, to society. Though loss may seem to hinder or slow our ability to give, it does not impede our growth or our impact on each other. Loss does not negate the process of nature nor our procession. It supports it.

Courage is a kind of salvation.

PLATO

We meet oppositions and temptations that threaten to distract us from our life's course and purpose. The greater the loss, the greater, it would seem, is the impediment in our path. But, no matter how forceful the winds of change are, nature, in her ever-honest presence, reminds us that beyond what we can see lies more to be seen. With endurance and a belief that transcends our limited view, we can look in that hopeful direction too. Many goodbyes that lead us to dramatic change blur or blind this view. Our task is to look ahead with faith in the future and trust eventual tomorrows to become clearer and directive.

Students of Goodbye

Goodbyes are our perennial teachers, instructing us to re-create our lives at every turn. They are hallmarks, indelibly placed guideposts stretched across the span of a lifetime to remind us where we have been, to lead us where we have yet to go. As we go, we take two universal and valuable lessons with us: the swiftness and unpredictability of time, and deepened compassion.

After the impact of loss, we realize how abruptly life can shift and how temporary today's reality is. The experience of goodbye can make us respect time more. A spotlight is placed on the here and now after loss, making us keenly aware of the present. Knowing that "now" will change, we come to cherish the present and live it in its momentary glory. Farewells teach us to become better livers of life as we approach it with a deeper respect and sensitivity than we had prior to our experience with meaningful departures.

Goodbye also teaches a lesson in compassion. It leads us to discern in others what we can now see and/or feel because of what we have lived through ourselves. Empathy surfaces when we have experienced loss of any kind. Having been through trials, we meet the sorrows and confusions of others with increased understanding, tolerance, and acceptance, for the pain and insecurity they feel has been our own. Even though reasons for goodbyes differ along with levels of sadness, we come to recognize the challenges they bring. They are mirrored in emotion.

While the goodbye experience is one that no other person in the world can understand except

A healthy experience of letting pain be pain is always a schooling in compassion. For when a person has suffered deeply even once and has owned that suffering, that person can never forget and never fail to recognize the pain of others.

MATTHEW FOX

the one going through it, the feelings goodbyes evoke resemble each other. These resemblances are the common ground on which we stand with others who are undergoing goodbyes. A certain solidarity forms after the fragmentation of goodbyes are lived and lived through. Goodbyes weave a tighter fabric for humanity to cover itself with. This strengthened garment serves to support us from beginnings through endings.

In the magnitudinal differences in nature, in life, lies wonder. To know only what we can be sure of is to know less than life's grandeurs, mercies, and intentions. Within the uncertainty life brings, comes the need to find a certainty. It can be found. Within ourselves. Found when changeful experiences are rooted in heart and mind and through which a stronger center inside of us is grown. From "here" we can go to "there," wherever there finds us. And we can know that the transitions of life bring with them fulfilling growth.

Life is a perpetual state of temporary permanence. This fact is affirmed by changeful goodbyes. Aware that change is constant, goodbyes teach us to become seasoned changers, to move with change, however smooth or awkward. As we do, we realize that without our willingness to move we would stand frozen in goodbye and not be pliable for the next hello.

There is a wisdom of the head, and . . . a wisdom of the heart.

CHARLES DICKENS

Nature requires movement to produce growth. To bring ourselves to be all we are meant to be, we are to move wherever and however seasons of change lead us. Whether led by force or by gentleness to follow a goodbye, change will take us from one place to ultimately guide us to reach the destination to ourselves.

For everything you have missed, you have gained something else; and for everything you gain, you lose something.

RALPH WALDO EMERSON

CHAPTER 8

In the End

I am going to talk with you about love today, which is life, and death; it is all the same thing.

ELISABETH KÜBLER-ROSS

Winding through a goodbye and the seasons of change lead to this lucid reality: In the end, as it was in the beginning, it is all about love—love lived out, love withheld, love hoped for, love lost. All we change for is, in essence, love. It is the best we can know between hellos and goodbyes. In-betweens give us the chance to experience love and to manifest it. Love does not end at an ending. Sometimes this is where it begins.

Manifesting itself in numerous ways, love's presence is always there. From the quick hellos exchanged with someone who departs too soon, to the long, rich hello shared in marriage, with a child, in a home, love is present. It shows itself in many colors and continues throughout dark winters into lighter springs. Love comes over and over through all seasons of life, through all seasons of change.

Goodbyes are not severe enough to disable love from healing us. Where need is great, so is love. A closed heart, an aching heart, may block its arrival. But any blockage love encounters is constructed by the mind, a mind often too weak for love's penetration.

Continually showering itself to grow life, love touches all. Some welcome its nourishment and seek it; others reject it. Still, every human being needs love. No person can live without it. If there is the slightest willingness to let love resolve issues and soothe the heart, that inkling is the opening through which love enters to begin its restorative work.

When love hurts us, paradoxically it is love that heals us. It leaves in one form, only to arrive in another. Whether in memories, renewed tenderness, new relationships, the peace of acceptance, the glory of the present—love reveals itself. It stays long after what has been is gone. Because it remains in spirit, physical separations do not put an end to love. They cannot. Love, real love, is far too creative and encompassing to limit its revelation to physical form. It is a living power—intense, omnipresent, without end—like God.

We live to love. Sometimes we do this with our eyes, our touch, our absence, our silence. Love takes many forms so it can be applied in many situations. Responding to the changes love requires of us, sometimes we are to be strong, sometimes weak; sometimes we sense when to hold on, when to let go; sometimes we need to speak, sometimes to be quiet. There are times to reach out, times to be still, times to say hello, times to say goodbye.

Love lives a life of its own. It has a heart and mind of its own, which operates independently of humans and in ways we do not always understand. But love operates through humans well

To love at all is to be vulnerable.

C. S. LEWIS

and generously. Love expresses itself knowingly and diversely and spans wide spiritual realms. Because love thrives spiritually and has no limits, a goodbye does not end love; it simply changes its form of presentation.

We are ever changing, evolving, learning—growing. Our journey through the world is comprised of a multitude of choices, feelings, interests, and relationships that transform, on a daily basis, the place we hold in the world. As we change, love changes, too, in order to keep pace with our growth. Love leads us to the truest understanding of itself, while we are brought to a clearer understanding of who we are.

When love changes its form, the relationship between those we love and those who love us changes. Some love is deepened, strengthened over time; this love sustains us and supports us. Some love is more casual, more free; we need this love too. Even when the love of some people is not in our lives for long, its presence, however ephemeral, has value that helps lead us to love's truest purpose for our lives.

When we have loved someone or something, love is never over, so neither is our sense of loss. The tears of change that flow down our hearts are tears signifying participation in life. Tears reveal our connection to someone or something else. We chose to love. Tears are not a sign of

Before we can honestly breathe the word "love" we must acquire a deeper understanding of the immortal hope that originally inspired it and the moral obligations that keep it alive.

JOSHUA LOTH LIEBMAN

weakness or embarrassment for men or women. Tears are water, a sign of life, an element necessary for growth. When shared, love changes and brings tears to the eyes, they are but symbols of our involvement in life. We have not fully lived unless we have known love, with its many facets ranging from joy to grief, ecstasy to devastation, fulfillment to emptiness.

Loving others throughout our lives is what makes up life. There is no other energy source that makes life more rewarding, fulfilling, enriching, encouraging than love. But, as we love others and are loved by them, we must remember that the form love takes to express itself will change. As we yield to that change, we preserve the best of what love has brought to us and keep our hands open to what it has yet to bring.

With understanding and openness, this is possible. With kindness toward ourselves and others, this can be. With love for ourselves and others, we will always be able to move in love's sensitive direction. Throughout the seasons of change, we can be grateful to love for coming into our lives, shaping us and touching us in a way nothing else ever could, and, finally, for giving us the courage to say goodbye and the strength to say hello.

And now these three remain: faith, hope and love. But the greatest of these is love.

1 CORINTHIANS
13:13 (NIV)

It may seem odd, even contradictory, to those who have journeyed through this book, to learn that, after all is said and done, there is no such thing as goodbye. We can say and write our farewells, but, because of bonds we made yesterday, to yesterday we are linked, making a true separation impossible. Once connected with someone or something, we are a part of them for life, and they are a part of us. Having given something of ourselves and having received something from another, exchanges were made and we were made by them—exchanges that molded our character and shaped our attitudes, defining who we are today.

The person we walk around identifying as "me" is really a compilation of our experiences—the persons, places, and things we have known—all added unto us. We don't define ourselves by ourselves. We can't. We are influenced—enriched or depleted—by whom and what we have known, and, thereby, defined by our experiences. Even though goodbyes indicate a parting, they cannot take what they imparted. Goodbyes are separations, divisions between then and now, that teach us to take the finest of yesterday's experience, leave the rest behind, and use the lessons the past taught and the strength it gave to support the present to its fullest measure.

Season to season, second to second, the majestic, complex, and profound cycle of life is at hand. Wherever the seasons find us, life and love are there. Between them is hope. With these dynamics to hold us, we can continue to unfold from goodbye to hello to experience all the seasons of our lives.

Bibliography

Angelou, Maya. *Wouldn't Take Nothing for My Journey Now*. New York: Bantam, 1994.

Bartlett, John. *Familiar Quotations*. Boston: Little, Brown & Company, Inc., 1992.

Block, Douglas. *I Am With You Always*. New York: Bantam, 1992.

Emerson, Ralph Waldo. *Self-Reliance*. New York: Bell Tower, 1991.

Gibran, Kahlil. *Sand and Foam*. New York: Alfred A. Knopf, Inc., 1926.

Goldberg, Natalie. *Writing Down the Bones*. Boston: Shambala Publications, Inc., 1986.

_____. *Wild Mind*. New York: Bantam, 1990.

Goldsmith, Joel S. *The Thunder of Silence*. New York: HarperCollins Publishers, 1961.

Gordon, Arthur. *A Touch of Wonder*. New York: Jove/The Berkley Publishing Group, 1974.

Girzone, Joseph F. *Never Alone*. New York: Doubleday, 1994.

Kübler-Ross, Elisabeth. *On Life After Death.* Berkeley: Celestial Arts, 1991.

Lane, Barry. *Writing as a Road to Self-Discovery.* Cincinnati: F & W Publications, 1993.

Lewis, C. S. *The Four Loves.* New York: Harcourt Brace and Co., 1960.

Lindbergh, Anne Morrow. *Gift From the Sea.* New York: Random House, 1977.

Loth Liebman, Joshua. *Peace of Mind.* New York: Simon & Schuster, 1946.

Lusser Rico, Gabriele. *Writing the Natural Way.* New York: J. P. Tarcher, Inc., 1983.

Moore, Thomas. *Soul Mates.* New York: HarperCollins Publishers, 1994.

Muir, John. *The Yosemite.* Boston: Houghton Mifflin, 1914.

Rupp, Joyce. *Praying Our Goodbyes.* Notre Dame, IN: Ave Maria Press, 1988.

Snow, Kimberly. *Writing Yourself Home: A Woman's Guided Journey of Self Discovery.* Berkeley: Conari Press, 1989.

The Holy Bible, King James Version. Lebanon, TN: Dugan Publisher, 1988.

The Holy Bible, New International Version. Copyright 1973, 1978, 1984 by International Bible Society. Used by permission of Zondervan Bible Publishers.

Ueland, Brenda. *If You Want to Write*. St. Paul, MN: Graywolf Press, 1983.

Viorst, Judith. *Necessary Losses*. New York: Ballantine, 1987.

Williams, Margery. *The Velveteen Rabbit*. New York: Doubleday & Company, 1975.

Williamson, Marianne. *A Return to Love*. New York: HarperCollins Publishers, 1992.

Woolf, Virginia. *A Room of One's Own*. Orlando, FL: Harcourt Brace Jovanovich, Inc., 1929.

Zinsser, William. *On Writing Well*. New York: HarperCollins Publishers, 1976.